School of Joy

A Workshop Project for Children

about Friendship and Good Relationships

Mariana Buric

Illustrated by Raluca Burcă

School of Joy: A Workshop Project for Children About Friendship and Good Relationships. Third edition. 2025.

Text copyright © Mariana Buric 2025

Illustrations copyright © Raluca Burcă 2025

All rights reserved.

Dear Educators and Parents,

I am pleased to propose a workshop for children, ages 5 to 11, designed to support your efforts in teaching little ones how to establish harmonious relationships with their peers, understand and embrace the values of friendship, and become reliable friends themselves.

Since all children love stories, the workshop will begin with a captivating tale—**"Hedgehog's Heart: A Tale of Friendship Across Lands."**

Together with the hedgehog, the children will uncover the mysteries of genuine friendship, which they will internalize through engaging activities and games. These activities can be organized at school, kindergarten, camps, or even at home throughout the year.

Together, we can help children enjoy their time spent together and build friendships that can last a lifetime

Mariana Buric

Workbook Contents

Introduction of the workshop's theme and the book 4

"Hedgehog's Heart. A Tale of Friendship Across Lands" 4

Interactive Reading 6

Debate on the topic of friendship, based on the content of the story read 33

The Friendship Dance 35

    (A moment of movement set to music) 35

Role Play: 36

    Encounter with the hedgehog Spikey 36

Craft a Gift for a Loved One (Real or Imaginary Friend): ... 37

    "Create Magic with What You Have!" 37

Proposals for games and activities aimed at fostering positive relationships and bonds of friendship 39

Closing Remarks 52

3 | SCHOOL OF JOY

Introduction of the workshop's theme and the book

"Hedgehog's Heart. A Tale of Friendship Across Lands"

Please find a potential presentation below, which can be tailored according to the children's ages:

"*Dear Children,*

Today, we're going to talk about a very special subject: Friendship. *We'll work together to answer some important questions like:* **Do we need friends? What does it mean to be a friend?** *And many more!*

But we won't be alone. I've invited a special guest, **Spikey!** *Spikey is a hedgehog and the main character from a lovely story called* **Hedgehog's Heart: A Tale of Friendship Across the Land.**

Together with Spikey, we'll discover many interesting things about friendship. So, are you ready to travel into the world of friendship? Let's get started! "

SPIKEY

Interactive Reading

Please find the story below. If the teacher or parent has the book in print or electronic format, it will be shared with the children.

Throughout the story reading, **we'll take brief pauses** to ask the children questions to keep them engaged and interested.

Within the story, you'll find some questions written in blue to guide these brief pauses.

Hedgehog's Heart

A Tale of Friendship Across Lands

by Mariana Buric

Spikey was an ever-so-shy hedgehog. He didn't have many friends. In fact, he actually had none.

Other animals his size would stay away from him, because of the spikes that jutted out at random from his body.

Spikey was afraid of those who were bigger than him. And there were no other hedgehogs in his home forest. They had all run away, afraid of the foxes.

Spikey had wanted to run too, but he was too slow because of his wounded leg. So, he learned to dodge and hide from the foxes.

He was having a hard time being by himself. His only joy was to look up at the sky at night. Stars amazed him. Spikey thought it must be so pretty up there among them, to have so many friends that you can't even count them all.

One day, Spikey mustered together all his courage and left his hole. "There has to be a friend for me out there in this big world. I must find him."

So, he set off, his only luggage an acorn, for when he would become hungry.

He was moving slowly, most of the time close to the trees, careful to not be attacked. He knew his way out of the forest, but beyond that, he had no idea where to go.

As he was walking, Spikey paid very close attention to everything he saw: old trees with twisted branches growing down, beautiful flowers popping out of the green grass on the forest floor, and insects flying around in a frenzy.

Then, he heard it—a trill so nice, like he had never heard before. He scouted the area. It was a nightingale! She was sitting in a tree, hidden amongst the leaves, singing with all her might, like all the forest beings were there, present at her concert.

Spikey stood still. The nightingale's song brought him so much joy! It was like the song was lifting him high, high up to the stars. And he was no longer alone but had thousands of friends.

"Thank you! You have a voice like no other!" he said to the bird, overcoming his shyness.

The nightingale gave him a curious look. She did not understand his tongue. But she gave him a gift. She sang one more song. And then flew off.

"She could have been an amazing friend," thought Spikey. "If only I had wings, too . . ."

The hedgehog jumped on his healthy leg several times, trying to see the nightingale again, but she had disappeared. He continued his journey looking for her. He heard a bird singing on the other side of the forest. He tried to imitate her voice, making long sounds, which he hoped would match the nightingale's trills. But he could only scare off some flies.

The NIGHTINGALE

Spikey was approaching the exit of the forest. His heart was in his boots and his feet began to tremble. What was waiting for him beyond the trees? It took all his courage to inch a few steps forward.

❖ Brief discussion: What do you suppose awaits Spikey beyond the forest? Who do you think he will encounter? Let's discover this together by delving further into the story!

Suddenly, a light so bright came over him, that he stopped abruptly and closed his eyes.

"What could this be?" he thought, a little frightened.

A gentle warmth enveloped him. He opened his eyes, squinting. It was the sun. He was seeing it for the first time. Until then, only a few rays had reached him through the branches of the trees. He smiled. The light gave him courage.

"The sun is such a warm friend," Spikey said to himself. He looked at the sun, holding a paw in front of his eyes. He jumped again on his healthy foot, up as high as possible to touch it. He would have loved to hug it, but he was just so far away!

He greeted the sun by raising the paw in the air. The sun in response sent playful rays through the hedgehog's spikes to light his way from the sky.

Before him, Spikey could see some hills covered in orchards.

"I wonder what's beyond them?"

He decided to find out. Panting, he went up most of the road. But then started feeling that he couldn't go any farther. He stopped in the middle of the climb to catch his breath. He was hungry, so he opened his acorn and started eating it.

Before he was finished, he found himself pushed in a rosebush. He curled into a ball.

"What's with this ugly hedgehog?" an angry voice said. "Is there no other place he could have stopped?"

It was a large ram, whom Spikey had cut off. Apparently, the ram had hit him with his hoof into the bush.

Spikey bounced back and came out of the bush.

The RAM

"A friend like him I would not like to have," he told himself as he looked back at the ram. "He didn't even let me apologize."

All Spikey's bones hurt, especially his foot. He looked down and saw that he had a thorn there.

"How strange! A plant that looks like me," he said about the rose bush.

"How do those spikes help you?" he asked it.

The plant twisted slowly in the wind without making a sound.

"We could be friends. I'm not afraid of your spikes at all," said the hedgehog.

But the rose bush was silent. Spikey looked at it closely. Nothing about its appearance could have a voice.

"If you still hear me, thank you for defending me from the ram," said the hedgehog. "I will always remember you."

The rosehip was bowing again in the wind in complete silence.

"Goodbye and so long," said Spikey.

He continued his journey, looking back. But where was this marvelous smell coming from? The rose bush had left him a gift between the spikes: a rosehip flower, so its scent would accompany him on the road ahead. Spikey couldn't see it, but he enjoyed its presence.

Finally, he made it to the top of the hill. Far away in the distance, he saw another sky that merged into the sky above. It was the sea. But Spikey had never seen it before. He set his mind on going to touch this second sky.

❖ Brief discussion: Do you think Spikey will reach the sea? Let's see together.

"Hey, wanna help me?" called a voice.

Spikey turned around.

"I'm Rin."

RIN, the RAT

The owner of the voice was a rat sitting on top of a pile of dried leaves and twigs.

"Do you know a spaceship mechanic?" asked the rat.

Spikey looked shyly towards him.

"Do you like it?" the rat asked.

"What?"

"My ship," said Rin, pointing to a pile of leaves.

Spikey did not know what a spaceship was.

"Interesting!"

"The only thing is that it won't fly."

"Are you sure that it's for real?" Spikey asked.

"Very real. Look, it can hold me. See?"

Rin was jumping on one leg to convince Spikey how solid his ship was. He slipped and came tumbling down.

"I am in great need of a mechanic," he said while getting up on his feet. "I most certainly want to get to the moon tonight."

Spikey couldn't help himself and burst into laughter.

Rin looked very offended.

"You seemed nice. I see I was wrong."

"Please forgive me. But I have never heard of a rat who could fly."

"That's because I am the first to do that."

"Maybe that's why," added Spikey cautiously.

"If I could reach the moon, I would bring it back to light up my hole."

Spikey did not know how to tell Rin, to not upset him again, that his idea sounded absurd.

"Don't you think that the moon might not fit in your hole?"

"I will build a bigger one."

"But what will happen to the other animals? Maybe they need something to light up their paths at night."

"They'll be left with the stars."

"But what about the humans?" Spikey tried again. "They might get upset."

"They have so many lightbulbs that they won't even notice something's missing from the sky. If you want to, you can pick a star. I'll take you on my ship. I think we can be friends."

"Thank you," Spikey answered, "but I have to keep going."

"Go where? Can't you see it's late? Stay over at my place. I'll postpone my flight till tomorrow."

Spikey hesitated but ended up staying. He watched as the rat tried his best to be a good host. Rin fed Spikey peanuts and made him a bed from willow tree branches. He gave him the prettiest room.

The hedgehog slept so well that in the morning he could no longer get out of bed. But the fuss outside disturbed him. He stepped out of the hole and his eyes narrowed.

Rin had mobilized all the rats from the surroundings to create the greatest invention in history: the ship that would touch the sky. It would have a huge mast built like a ladder you could climb up to be the neighbor of the stars.

"Who has heard of such a strange thing before?" the skeptics said, surprised.

But Rin had great powers of persuasion. He had promised them all that they would be able to bring on the earth as many stars as they would like to illuminate their holes.

Rin in His Dreamworld

SCHOOL OF JOY

"He's an innovator. Let's follow him," said the old rats. "We'll get our nation out of the darkness!"

They all went to work diligently—more than the ants. They gathered everything in their way to pick up the huge ship in the sky; leaves, bits of wood, stones, grass, even dried mushrooms. Rin was just fidgeting around and giving instructions. When they saw Spikey the rats suddenly got upset.

"Who's this odd thing?" they asked each other. "Leave immediately," they said to Spikey.

The hedgehog shriveled and would have made himself invisible at that moment.

"It's my friend!" Rin said in his defense. "Please be polite to him."

But the other rats could not be convinced.

"The sky is ours. We don't want to share it with strangers," they shouted.

And they began to declare themselves owners over the Big Dipper, the Small Dipper, the North Star, some of them even over entire galaxies.

"You know, I love the stars too," said Spikey in a whisper.

But no one noticed him.

"Please leave at least one star in the sky, the smallest one, just so I can look at her," he pleaded.

But even Rin ignored him. He was too concerned with not losing the Moon.

Spikey looked at the rats, horrified. He could not imagine such a dark night in which the sky was emptied of stars. He had to do something to stop them. But how? How? He was alone, and there were so many of them! He took his heart into his mouth and began to speak again.

"Forgive me," said the hedgehog so loudly that his voice echoed in the rats' ears.

They fell silent and gazed at him. Spikey looked into their eyes with courage he did not know he had.

"Have you thought that you could fall off the ladder from carrying so many stars?" he asked them.

The rats gaped at each other. No. They hadn't thought about that. In their hurry to raise the ship, they had missed that.

"What if the ladder breaks?" continued Spikey.

They hadn't thought of that, either.

"We could have an accident," said Rin.

"Or we could even die," considered another rat.

"We need an engineering solution," was the opinion of the Elders. "But where do we find an engineer?"

There had been no one in their country. He had to be found somewhere else. But no one would dare to make such a journey. Then they made a suggestion to Spikey. If he found the engineer, they would leave a star in the sky for him.

"You know, I think the stars and the moon are for all the creatures of the earth," he said.

"Don't be naive. They are for those who reach them first," argued Rin.

"It means they are for us," the other rat reinforced.

Spikey could not be convinced. He did not want to be a star thief. So he said goodbye, and he carried on with his journey.

"We'll manage without you," the rats cried out. "You'll be sorry!"

- ❖ Brief conversation: Do you believe Spikey will ultimately find a friend? Why do you hold that belief? Let's discover this together!

But the hedgehog was very glad to have ruined their plans. He looked at the sky. The sun was there, as it had been all the days before, and it was warming him with its rays. He welcomed it, raising a paw. Smiled. He knew he had a friend. Even if it was so far away.

Spikey had been walking through the heat all day, and still, he had not reached the sea. He had stopped only once to admire a peacock. The loveliest of colors were painted on his feathers. He had a huge tail that he would elegantly move. Other birds would stand around him, trying to win his favor.

"Hi! My name is Spikey," said the hedgehog, approaching the peacock, fascinated by his beauty.

But the peacock didn't notice him.

"Hey, I'm glad to meet you!" insisted the hedgehog, making a sign with his paw.

But the peacock had eyes for no one but himself. He walked around, puffing up his feathers, and saying to himself that he was the most beautiful bird on earth.

The hedgehog became sad. He wanted the peacock to give him just a glance. He was so close! If the peacock wanted, Spikey would have been his best friend, but he didn't.

The **PEACOCK**

"It is hard to be friends with someone who does not want to see me," thought the hedgehog. So he moved on.

The sun was about to go down, and Spikey was still on his way. Hunger got the best of him. The hedgehog had not come across any mushrooms as he had hoped he would. In vain, he had run after a mosquito, but he did not manage to catch it.

The sea was close, but the hedgehog had not the strength to get to it.

Spikey came across a small garden and thought to do what he did best—to clean it of caterpillars. So he crawled under the fence and got to work. Not half an hour had passed, and all the caterpillars were gone. Into his belly!

As he was resting under an old walnut tree, Spikey saw two silhouettes with watering cans on their backs approaching.

"Boy, we are free tonight," said the owner of the garden to his son, David. "It looks like someone else did our job for us."

"Look! There's our sanitarian, Dad!" The kid said, picking up Spikey. "He is so beautiful!" The boy gently stroked his back, not at all afraid of his spikes.

The hedgehog blushed and dared not make a sound.

DAVID and SPIKEY

"Then let him stay with us," the father responded. "A skilled sanitarian is a blessing in any house."

The boy gave Spikey a slice of watermelon and built him a nest in the back of the garden.

"Good night!" he said while stroking Spikey's nose. "See you tomorrow."

Spikey did not understand the words but could feel the child's love. And that made him happy. So happy that he could not fall asleep.

He started counting the stars, as he would do every night. The moon was up again. Rin had not managed to bring it to his hole. That meant that the moon could guide his way in the dark. He still had a dream! And he was so close to making it come true. Spikey went on the road again without a moment's hesitation.

The sound of the waves caressed his hearing and his nostrils filled with salty air. Spikey struggled to advance through the sand, stumbling over the many shells. He fell and rose again. One more step! One more step! Until he reached the end of his journey.

"It is a moving sky," he said. "And full of water. But who could this be?"

Spikey moved his head a little. As he was going back and forth, the image followed him.

"What a funny hairdo he has!" and started laughing.

The image in the water was laughing, too. Slowly, Spikey realized it was a reflection of himself. He looked nothing like the peacock, the rat, the ram, or the nightingale. He was just a hedgehog, like all hedgehogs that had run from the foxes. But . . . why did he have two heads? A second face appeared in the water, smiling at him.

"How about a swim?"

Spikey turned around, confused. It had been a while since he last heard anyone speaking his tongue.

"Come on, join me," urged a plump hedgehog while he was jumping in the water. "The name's Dimi, by the way."

Spikey followed Dimi into the watery second sky. But just as soon as he started, he slipped on a rock and sank. Dimi quickly jumped to his rescue and brought him to shore.

"Why didn't you say you don't know how to swim?" Dimi asked.

Spikey didn't answer. He was too scared. He had swallowed a lot of water. And his mouth had turned incredibly salty.

"It's so simple. You just move your feet and the water keeps you afloat. If you wanna, I can teach you."

SPIKEY Meets DIMI

"Maybe some other time," Spikey said. "I am tired now."

"I know a many-starred hotel," Dimi joked, showing him a sand dune under the starry sky. "There's room for you too."

The plump hedgehog pointed to a dune in the open air.

"That's it?" wondered Spikey.

"Yes. Isn't it wonderful? At night, you can count the stars from your bed."

"Amazing! But I do get cold fairly easily. In my forest, I used to have a hole."

Spikey started missing the places he had left behind again. He almost started crying.

"I used to have a hole once too," replied Dimi. "We were five brothers and we all lived together. It was so nice. But one day, a boat came ashore. We decided we would leave with it. We were curious to see what is there beyond the sea. But . . . „

Dimi became silent. His eyes drifted somewhere in the direction of the sea.

"I wanted to play with the butterflies one more time. And I got off the ship. There were so many of them that morning. They were flying over me, and I kept trying to touch them. I didn't hear the boat's engine start. When I realized it, my brothers were already long gone."

"I am sorry. But I understand you. I once loved a butterfly too," said Spikey. "He was small and yellow with blue spots. So beautiful! But I lost him by nightfall. He had gone to the kingdom of butterflies."

"I think the same happened to my butterflies," Dimi said. "I don't even know when they disappeared. And since then, I've stayed here, waiting . . . and waiting . . . for another ship, so I can get to my brothers. I don't know why, but no ships come to shore anymore."

"You and I, we are much alike," replied Spikey.

Then Spikey shared his own story of sadness with Dimi. When he was finished, Dimi looked at him.

"We could be friends."

"That would make me happy," said Spikey. "But it's hard for me to sleep here. If you wanted to, I know of a garden. A generous boy made a nest for me there."

Dimi looked pleased. "You'll have me over?"

"Well," Spikey said, "are we not friends?"

From that day forward, the two were inseparable. Spikey overcame his fear and learned how to swim. Swimming helped him walk again after hurting his leg when he ran away, afraid of the foxes. He wasn't even that shy anymore. He liked to race the dolphins. They would catapult him in the air, and he'd somersault in the sea like an acrobat, entertaining the gardener's boy. David had grown fond of the two hedgehogs. He made a nest for Dimi, right next to Spikey's.

At night, they would all look to the sky. The boy had a telescope and dreamt of becoming an astronaut. And Spikey and Dimi hoped he would take them with him when he would travel through the stars.

❖ Brief conversation: Did you like the story? What did you like the most?

The End

Debate on the topic of friendship, based on the content of the story read

Please find below a set of possible questions for this debate:

1. Why was Spikey looking for friends?
2. But why do people need friends?
3. What does it mean for you to be friends with someone?
4. Why couldn't Spikey befriend the nightingale? What about the sun?
5. What made Spikey not want to be friends with the ram? Could you have a friend who behaves like the ram? Why? But what would you have done if you were in the ram's place and met Spikey?
6. What qualities did Spikey appreciate in Rin the hedgehog? But why couldn't he choose him as a friend? What would you have done if you were in Spikey's place? Why?

7. What prevented Spikey from befriending the peacock? Could you be friends with someone who ignores you? Why?
8. How did Spikey become friends with David, the gardener's boy? Why do you think David and Spikey liked each other?
9. How did Spikey become friends with Dimi? Why do you think the two hedgehogs chose to be friends forever?
10. What qualities would you like your friends to have?
11. What do you think about yourselves, can you be good friends? What do you like to share with friends and what don't you like? Have you ever argued with your friends? How did you reconcile? If you could change something in your behavior to be better friends, what would you change? How do you think your classmates, teachers, or parents could help you be good friends?
12. What is the difference between a person's friendship with another person and a person's friendship with an animal?

The Friendship Dance

(A moment of movement set to music)

Children will be invited to participate in a brief dance session to a song they enjoy: "Before we proceed, I suggest we engage in a bit of movement. Some of you might already be familiar with the Friendship Song. Let's listen to it and dance together."

Role Play:

Encounter with the hedgehog Spikey

Please find a potential scenario below:

"Imagine that you come across Spikey and wish to form a friendship with him. Introduce yourselves and share three things that you believe are the most significant about you." (For instance: My name is Alex. I am 6 years old. I enjoy bike rides, fried potatoes, and cartoons featuring . . .)

Craft a Gift for a Loved One (Real or Imaginary Friend):

"Create Magic with What You Have!"

1. Equipped with just a sheet of paper, writing tools, and colored pencils, the children are invited to create a heartfelt gift for a friend. This could be a drawing, an origami craft, a greeting card, a letter, and so on. The possibilities are only limited by each child's imagination. Children will be encouraged to be as original as possible in crafting their gifts.

2. For preschool children, the following activity can be implemented: "The Mischievous Hedgehog."
Each child will receive a coloring sheet that features the black and white (outline) image of the character Spikey. They will be encouraged to color it using the favorite colors of their friend (real or imaginary). Depending on the colors chosen, the images can turn out to be quite amusing and bring joy to the children.

Proposals for games and activities aimed at fostering positive relationships and bonds of friendship

1. The Friendship Greeting

At the beginning and end of classes, children will be encouraged to greet each other using **traditional forms of salutation** that embody the concept of friendship, **or** they can create **a unique salutation for their class**. A brainstorming session can be conducted where children will be asked what elements they would like to incorporate in this salutation. Together, they will select the salutation that they deem most appropriate, ensuring it respects diverse opinions and includes every child.

Possible examples:

> Friendship Smiles: Children will smile at each other while holding their fingers together in front of them, forming a heart shape. They can say phrases like: "I'm happy to see you!", "Sunshine in the heart!", or "I'm here for you!"

The Circle of Friendship: Children will extend their arms and cross them in front of their bodies, creating a circle. They can express a short wish such as: "Joy in unity!" or "Success!"

Friendship Fists: Children will clench their fists and gently bump them against their classmates. They can express small wishes like: "Let's have a wonderful day together!" or "Success!" and so on.

The Embrace of Joy: Children will approach each other and embrace at the shoulders, forming a circle. They can collectively express a wish such as: "We won't give up! We learn together!"

Say, **"Thank you for today! Eager to see you tomorrow!"**

At the end of classes, children will express gratitude for the time spent together and share their anticipation of seeing each other again.

The purpose of these greetings is to ensure each child feels accepted and warmly received by their peers, fostering a joyful attitude towards attending kindergarten or school. Moreover, these greetings contribute to an enthusiastic atmosphere in the classroom, which positively impacts the learning process.

2. Establishing the Rules of Friendship in the Joyful Classroom

The educator will explain to the students that they will participate in a game through which they can set their own rules for good conduct in their class. This will take into account how they would like to be treated by their peers and the qualities and behaviors that a true friend should exhibit (for example: kindness, respect, politeness, compassion, active listening, helpfulness, love, generosity, altruism, etc.)

- Children will be asked to take turns expressing **how they would like their classmates to interact with them in various life scenarios**. For instance, if they are upset about receiving a poor grade, if they are excited about scoring a goal in a soccer match or solving a challenging math problem, if they've had a fall and torn their pants, if they are new to the class and don't know anyone, or if they are wearing glasses for the first time and feel self-conscious because they think they don't look good, and so on.
- As each child responds to the questions, **the educator will assist them in conceptualizing the value or behavior described** and will record

it on the board or on a large sheet of paper displayed on an easel, ensuring it is visible to all children.

- Ultimately, children will be encouraged to reach a consensus on the good behavior rules they wish to implement in their classroom.

- Trustworthy Friends! (Mini-Drama)
  - Children will be divided into groups of 2-3 and will be tasked with creating a mini-drama based on a real or imaginary event that incorporates one of the Friendship Rules they have established (each group leader will randomly select a rule). Once the groups have prepared their mini-dramas, they will be asked to perform them in front of the class.

3. Self-Discovery and Mutual Discovering Through Play

- "If You Were . . ." This game is designed to bring to light the self-perception of the children. They will also discover that they share common preferences with their classmates for certain plants, animals, etc., which can strengthen their connections. Each child will be asked by their peers what they would like to be if they were an entity from the plant or animal world, or from the world of arts or music, and why they made that choice.

Examples of questions could be:

- If you were a bird, what kind would you want to be? Why?
- If you were a flower, what would your name be? Why?
- If you were a melody, which one would you be? Why?
- If you were a character from a story, who would you choose to be? Why?
- If you were a musical instrument, which one would you want to be? Why?

- The Communication Bridge: This game is designed to enhance children's skills in listening, attention, clear communication, and collaboration.
  - Participants will be split into two teams positioned face-to-face. They will be instructed that they need to construct an imaginary bridge from 10 logs, which will be completed once the 10 communication challenges (each symbolizing a log) are resolved.

- Each team will receive a list of 5 words or phrases that signify communication barriers. Examples include: smile, respect, help, compassion, uninterrupted listening, gratitude, joy, friend, hug, gift.
- Each team is required to use a variety of communication methods to relay their message (such as gestures, facial expressions, drawings, body language, etc.)
- Once all communication hurdles have been overcome, the children from both teams join their raised arms while standing face-to-face, symbolizing a bridge. They can choose to sing a beloved song to express their joy of having successfully built a bridge of communication.

4. The Week of Smiles

Throughout this week, children will participate in various games centered around the theme of "smile".

They will be encouraged to smile a lot and observe the impact of their smiles on themselves and those around them. They will discover that a smile is a delightful form of communication, which can be a priceless gift.

The Seekers of Smiles and Statues

- The kids will be split into two groups: "Smile Seekers" and "Statues."
- The "Statues" will position themselves in a specific area, remaining still and serious.
- The "Smile Seekers" are tasked with making the "Statues" smile. They can use jokes, mimicry, amusing dances, or any other gesture that might elicit a smile, but they are not allowed to touch the "Statues."
- If a "Statue" ends up smiling or laughing, they will join the "Smile Seekers" and will attempt to make the remaining "Statues" smile.
- The game concludes when all the "Statues" have either smiled or laughed.

The Chain of Smiles

This is a method to educate children about the power of a smile and how it can bring joy not only to the giver but also to the receiver.

- One child will be selected to initiate the game. This child will bestow a broad smile upon another peer. The recipient of the smile must then pass it on by smiling at someone else. The game proceeds until everyone has both received and passed on a smile.

Children will be urged to notice how the smile propagates and alters the mood of those in its path.

The Smile Journal

- Each child receives a "Smile Journal," which can be a special, beautifully colored notebook that they enjoy writing in.
- Kids are encouraged to smile at as many people as they can outside of school - this includes friends, family members, neighbors, and even strangers (but only under adult supervision in the latter case).
- In their diary, the children will record the person they smiled at, the reaction they received, and how it made them feel. At the conclusion of the week, the children have the opportunity to share their experiences with their classmates.

5. Activities to Promote Good Deeds and Gratitude

- ### The Kindness and Gratitude Circle
  - A circle will be created with all the students in the class.
  - The students will be instructed that each of them should mention a kind act that another classmate or person has performed for them, for which they are genuinely thankful. They will be encouraged to express their appreciation to that person.

- o The activity will proceed in a clockwise manner until each student has shared their personal experience.
- **Heartfelt Gifts**
- o Kids will be encouraged to donate personal belongings (such as books, toys, clothes, etc.) to less fortunate children.
- o They will be guided to select the gift with care, ensuring it is in good condition, clean, and attractively wrapped. They will also be motivated to write a letter or a greeting card for the recipient of the gift, expressing their delight in giving and a sincere message for the recipient.
- o Depending on the circumstances, the gifts are distributed by schools, NGOs, parents, or even by the children themselves.

6. The Circle of Forgiveness

This activity can be arranged daily or weekly, depending on the circumstances and requirements. Its purpose is to ensure that children do not end their school day harboring resentment towards each other, but instead, try to resolve minor conflicts promptly to avoid accumulating grievances and frustrations.

- A circle will be created with all the students in the class.

- The students will be informed about the importance of sincere and open communication. They will be invited to share if anything in their relationships with their classmates is bothering them. The children will be encouraged to take turns speaking, to do so respectfully, and to attentively listen to each other.
- The game will continue in a clockwise direction until each child shares their own experience.
- If certain children struggle with openly expressing their feelings, they will be encouraged to write letters to each other, sharing their concerns and feelings about the situation. They can choose to read these letters in the Forgiveness Circle, or they may opt to simply exchange them privately among themselves. Classmates should be urged to respect each other's privacy and not attempt to discover the contents of the letters.

7. Helping Each Other, We Learn Together

The activities in this chapter are designed to foster team spirit and teach children about generosity, patience, and constructive dialogue.

- **The Most Beautiful Book Read** (Presentation and Sincere Debates): Students will be asked to give a brief presentation about the most beautiful book they have ever read. After each presentation, the listeners will be required to provide reasoned feedback about what they liked and what they didn't like about the presentation. They will be reminded to be sincere and polite, and it will be emphasized that this approach will help their peers to continually improve their presentations.

- **The Teacher and The Student:** This game encourages more advanced children to help those who need assistance, promoting empathy, patience, and communication skills.
    - The children will be divided into pairs, a "teacher" and a "student". The teacher is a child who has more advanced knowledge about the chosen subject (for example: solving a math exercise, drawing an object, completing a puzzle, etc.)
    - The teacher helps their student to learn or make progress in learning the chosen subject.
    - After a predetermined period of time, the learning topics and the roles of the children are switched.

8. Together, on Your Birthday!

For their birthdays, children can create small, self-made surprises for their classmates. Here are a few examples:

- **The Box of Positive Thoughts**
  - Each child in the class is asked to write down a quality they admire in each of their classmates or a well-wish for them.
  - These will be written on colorful notes and placed in special boxes.
  - On their birthday, each child will receive the box prepared specifically for them. This gesture will make them feel valued and loved by their peers, bringing them joy.

- **The Friendship Puzzle**
  - Each child will be asked to contribute a piece to the puzzle that is being prepared for the birthday child. The small puzzle pieces can include drawings, special messages, stickers, or photos that represent their friendship, etc.
  - On their birthday, the birthday child will receive a completed puzzle composed of all the pieces contributed by their classmates (for example: a heart, a ball, the birthday child's favorite toy/object, etc.)

This symbolic gift will not only bring joy and serve as a pleasant memory for the birthday child, but it will also foster connections among the children and strengthen their team spirit.

- **FRIENDSHIP DAY - JULY 30th**

Even though most children are on vacation during this day, a camp could be arranged, or meetups could be organized with small groups of friends at home, in a park, at a bakery, or at a playground. This way, children can celebrate their friendship.

A special guest at this event could be an actor dressed as Spikey the Hedgehog. This guest will engage the children in fun games and dance moments while also leading interesting discussions about friendship.

Closing Remarks

Thank you so much for taking the time to go through the content of this workshop project.

I hope it assists or at least inspires you in your endeavors. In a world that's becoming increasingly fraught with conflict, children need all of us, particularly parents and educators, to learn about good relationships and friendship, and to achieve mental and emotional balance. Certainly, my approach is a drop in the ocean, but I believe that together with you, the good thought can bear fruits.

I hope that more and more children will leave kindergarten and school, not only with the memory of dear people but also with principles and values that will instill in them strong character and the ability to live with dignity, regardless of the circumstances.

With Gratitude,

Mariana Buric

http://joyinwords.com

joy.in.words.stories@gmail.com

NOTES

NOTES

NOTES

NOTES

NOTES

NOTES

NOTES

_____

_____

_____

_____

_____

_____

_____

_____

_____

_____

_____

_____

_____

_____

NOTES

NOTES

NOTES

NOTES

NOTES

NOTES

NOTES

NOTES

NOTES

NOTES

NOTES

NOTES

NOTES

NOTES

NOTES

NOTES

_____
_____
_____
_____
_____
_____
_____
_____
_____
_____
_____
_____
_____
_____

Made in the USA
Las Vegas, NV
05 May 2025